Torn

Blue October

Presentation by *BookLeaf Publishing*

Web: www.bookleafpub.com

E-mail: info@bookleafpub.com

ISBN: 9789395756785

First edition 2022

DEDICATION

To the other half of my soul, from my demons to yours

PREFACE

They were always drawn to each other yet pulled apart by life and morals. They didn't know they were twin flames that never had a chance, that they pushed each other to grow, to construct and deconstruct, to go high and go inside as deep as they could be. They killed and resurrected love and hate and hope again and again, but they would have to wait for another lifetime to find their happiness. This is a glimpse into a history of tears and love for two tormented souls looking for each other and never finding the way.

Us

We connected through fun
Drinking shots, staying late
Young fools playing games
With the fate
Never thought you're the one

We connected through laughter
Telling jokes no one could
Have understood
But us two
I thought that's what you're after

Through the music we danced
Never long in one place
Going high, going low
Everything in between
We were deeply romanced

Our bodies started reacting
On the beach, in the mountains
We pushed through
It all
But we started the acting

When we discovered the wit
We would flirt mind to mind

We were one
Of a kind
Turning it all into art

So we started saving each other
Angel and demon, trading places
Starting races
That left us bruised and broken
We shouldn't have bothered

Because when we connected in pain
Through gazes and songs
And looks that could
Both love and kill
I waged war on myself
As I tried to remain
True to myself
So it wasn't a game, no it wasn't a game
Yet it killed me the same, it killed me the same...

Torn

Torn
Between the want and the must
Between the would and the should
Just the old battle
Between the soul and the mind
Every molecule
Split in halves
Pushing each other
Running both towards and away
Could you ever imagine
Living like that?
And yet I must...

*

The impossible choice
What to do, to take which way
When they hurt me both the same
To love you is to hate me
To lose you is a sin
And I'll hate myself if I do
And I'll hate myself if I don't
Oh the conundrum I'm in

*

Divided

In halves and quarters
percentages that don't matter
Because I'm still divided
And can dream
Or do math
But I can never be
A whole

Vicious cycle

For your pain
I got off my high horse
And I stumbled
I walked over myself
And I bled
Threw caution to the wind
And I burned

So I cried myself
Into someone else
As I died
Only to be reborn
Still thinking of you
But can I risk
What's left of my sanity
For you

I always do…

The Beast

I tried to show you
How much
I cut me open
To the bones
To let you in
And then
She started trashing
Her tail
To wreak havoc
And make sure
I wasn't loved
And I wish
You'd have seen
How she's my jailer
And how she does it
Out of a terrible fear
Of being hurt
Because she knows
That's where it always ends
And I wish
You walked past her
To me

Confusion

What the hell are you asking
And what the fuck am I saying
That we ended up here
Where both of us die
In different ways

And at this point
Either I
didn't understand the question
Or you the answer
But it doesn't matter anymore
Because I don't need to understand
Beyond the blood
pouring from the bites
You leave on me
Whenever you're in pain
Never seeing
It's of your own doing
Still choosing
To believe
The worst of me

And I fuckin spliced for you

Behind the wall

You believe the ones I show
When surrounded
Never waiting for the other me
The one who's only for your eyes to see
Quick to get the no
When the yes is too slow
'Cause you don't know
How big
The dam is

Never giving a chance to respond
You see what you want
And you make up your mind
Then show me your pain
To shoot once again
Me down

I'll drown
Just like the other times
And just like then
I will come back to life
But this time
Not to you…

Morbid dance

There's a big difference
Between the 'won't' and the 'can't'
Or is there
When the price is the same
Measured
In tears and fake smiles
And pieces of us
That disappear
Never to be seen again
And there's not enough music
To drown away the screams
Of our mutilated souls
So take
Another bite of me
While I chew
The last of you
And no one can see
That I'm turning into you
And you're becoming me

Carousel

You drown
And I jump at the chance
To help once again
Returning the favor
And we dance
To the music we make
Made anew
Then you ask
And I scream
It cuts me in new places
Every time
Half nightmare
half my dream
Not mine to have
Yet feel you mine
I still say no
Although I know
It kills us both
And we get back
On the carousel
And every time
my no slowly dies
But you can't hear
The yes

When it comes

The Mask

I whispered
Take your mask off
Mine is
And you didn't hear me
I yelled
take your mask off
Mine is
And you didn't want to
You sang
Take your mask off
Mine is
And I couldn't
As I was screaming
Behind the mask
You caged me in

…I cried
Take your mask off
And the only answer
Was the echo
Of an empty heart…

Sacrifice

I knew we'd mess up
One way or another
Because you were more raw
Than ever before
And I was tons crazier
Than the one you loved
So I had to give her
Some of my spark
Some of my crazy
The light kind
That you liked in me
To translate to her
Some of your flaws
Into the strengths
They really were
To teach her
How to love you
And stop killing you
Because I couldn't
Leave you
For another century
Unloved
When we messed up
Like we always do

History

First
He loved her like a boy
And like a girl
She laughed
Then
He loved her like a man
And like a woman
She cried
And last
He loved her like an old man
And like an old woman
She died

Behind the wall II

He never knew of the waves inside her
Crashing and breaking her
Of the sacrifices she made
Her broken mind trying to comprehend
Hurting whenever she hurt him
Because she couldn't understand
He never knew of the ocean of love
Trying to break through her walls
They were the shore and the sea
Running to and away from each other
Just as she always thought
They saw a six and a nine
Or maybe a comma or apostrophe
When they were actually seeing
The same is it or could it be

Late

Late
One of us
is always too late
Too late to show pain
To late to understand
To show
To forgive
To feel
To scream
Too late
For both love and hate
I'm sorry
I didn't understand
Sooner
And that you didn't understand
I was coming
From very far
Away

Difference

The difference is
You talked
Like they were all
Stupid
And I answered
Like they were all smart
The difference is
I ran
To your pain
While you fed
On mine
The difference is
I thought
The best of you
While you thought
The worst of me
The difference is
I can't fix myself
This time
While you
Already did
So I can only
Hope to learn
To love myself
The way I am

The way you didn't

The Monster

So many people
Took so many bites
Out of me
When I look in the mirror
I don't recognize
who I see
They made me a monster
They made me insane
Or maybe they just revealed the inside
And I got only myself to blame

Killers

The truth is
I'm so crazy
It would be a crime
To let you love me
But I did
So here we are
I'm hunted by my inner police
And you're wherever the fuck you are

It's true
Sometimes you kill me
Sometimes I kill you

Not Enough

At first
we were
too stupid to understand
And then
at times we were
too scared to admit it
too honest not to fight it
too proud to accept it
too weak to oppose it
too hurt to try again
too in love to give up
Too much
Too much
So much
Yet in the end
Still not enough

I

*

I had
To put myself together
So many times because of you
I look
Like a fuckin Picasso
If only
I'd be priceless
Too…

**

I thought
I knew
A thing or two
Of pain and love.
Then I met you

* * *

I try so hard
To climb my walls
Only to discover
I can't
Break down yours

* * * *

I built
My walls
From the rocks
You've been throwing
At me

Choice

When I'm high
I choose you
When I'm down
I choose you
When I'm torn,
when I'm sane,
when I'm crazy,
when I'm lame
I choose you!!
I chose you over him
Over her
Over me

Why the fuck couldn't you see…

Metamorphosis

Like a fuckin moth
Drawn to your flame
My wings long gone
I crawl
Why do I still believe
You could be good for me
Wingless as I am
Just hoping
It's all part of the metamorphosis
Needed
To make us
One

Death of the Phoenix

*

To give up
I can't
It would break my heart
Like every time
I tried before

To give in
I can't
It would break my mind
Like every time
I tried before

So since I'm breaking
Anyway
Instead of going
Should I stay
Out of my mind
Or without a heart
Those are my choices
I can't leave it at that

So I take the plunge
And I crash
No longer fire

Only ash

www.ingramcontent.com/pod-product-compliance
Lightning Source LLC
Chambersburg PA
CBHW060926130726
48001CB00006B/2443